Body Blips,
Blips,
Wobbly Bits
and
Great BIG Zits

About the author

Anita Naik is a writer and columnist. She is the author of over thirty books on everything from beauty secrets to fitness, self esteem and health. She is also the former agony aunt of *Just 17* and *Closer* magazines, and the current agony aunt on *TV Quick*. For more information, go to www.anitanaik.co.uk

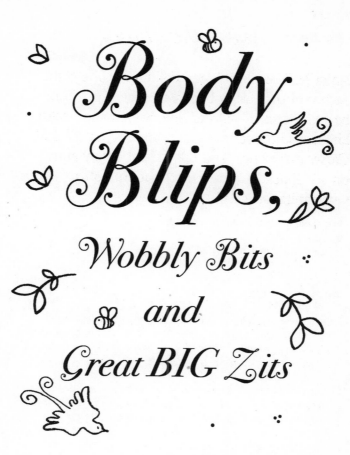

Body Blips,
Wobbly Bits
and
Great BIG Zits

Anita Naik

PICCADILLY PRESS • LONDON

For Bella

First published in Great Britain in 2007
by Piccadilly Press Ltd,
5 Castle Road, London NW1 8PR

A catalogue record for this book is available from
the British Library

ISBN 978 1 85340 909 7

1 3 5 7 9 10 8 6 4 2

Printed and bound in Great Britain by Bookmarque Ltd
Cover design by Simon Davis
Book design by Fiona Webb

Contents

Introduction

Dear God,
Please give me long, slim legs, a tiny waist,
athletic arms, long hair that doesn't frizz in
the rain, clear glowing skin (definitely no zits,
please), nails that don't break and a belly
that never gets fat, no matter how many
cakes and chocolate bars I eat!

If only! Hands up if you've wished for all or at least some of the above? Or longed to look in the mirror and see someone who actually liked her body and herself? And who can blame you? Wouldn't life just be so much easier if chocolate made you thin, or if lying on the sofa watching *The OC* made you fitter, or if you really could just wish yourself gorgeous and wake up feeling it?

Well, the truth is, you *can* wish yourself gorgeous. Maybe not in the way you think. You can't wake up two dress sizes smaller or three inches taller. But this book explains how being gorgeous is within your power – and shows you how to make it happen!

Feeling Good About Yourself

*'Sometimes I hate the way I look and feel
like crying, then other days I think, "No,
I'm actually OK and really quite pretty."
My feelings about myself change all the time.'*

Sophie

This chapter is all about what makes you tick,
inside and out. How you feel about your body
affects everything else in your life. If you hate your
looks, you're guaranteed to go through life feeling
horrible. You'll become an expert at holding

yourself back because you don't feel good enough, or nice enough, or pretty enough. You'll feel ugly when you look in the mirror, you'll hide in corners at parties and keep quiet at school, and you'll imagine that, compared to everyone else, you're just not worthy.

You need to learn to feel good about yourself. Luckily, this isn't about mad diets, giving up your favourite treats or begging your parents for plastic surgery. It's about getting real with who you are right now. This doesn't mean you have to accept everything about yourself. You can work wonders through healthy eating and exercise (see Chapter 2 for more on this), and you can learn to deal with all kinds of body blips (see Chapter 3) and kick any horrible habits (see Chapter 4). But to be truly happy, you have to stop trying to be perfect, and start liking the real YOU.

If you see yourself as a waste of space with a body to be ashamed of, that's how you'll act and feel. But if you see yourself as someone strong and interesting with a body in a million, that's exactly who you'll be. Sounds impossible? Keep reading!

Your Secret Self Quiz 1

How Do You Really Feel About Yourself?

1. When you look in a mirror your first reaction is that:
   a. you're OK (5)
   b. you're disgusting (0)
   c. you're looking good (10)

2. Sometimes you secretly worry that:
   a. you're not a very nice person (5)
   b. you'll never get a boyfriend (10)
   c. everyone hates you (0)

3. The thought of standing up in class makes you feel:
   a. sick – you hate people looking at you (0)
   b. scared – it makes you nervous (5)
   c. annoyed – it means you have to pay attention (10)

4. If someone gives you a compliment you:
   a. assume they're just being nice (0)
   b. assume they want something (5)
   c. assume it's true (10)

5. When someone says something mean to you, you:
   a. pretend it doesn't matter and then cry in private (5)
   b. get angry with them (10)
   c. assume it's true and never forget it (0)

3

6. What do you like most about yourself?
- a. nothing (0)
- b. my sense of humour (5)
- c. most things (10)

Now total your scores.

0 – 15 Secretly insecure

Your self-esteem is seriously flagging and needs rescue work. Right now you feel horrible about yourself so you need to work on your strengths and stop fixating on your weaknesses. Keep reading to find out how.

20 – 40 Secretly scared

You have fairly good self-esteem but it needs work, because you often doubt yourself and your abilities, and you let others decide who you are. Remember, you are your own boss, so act like it! There are loads of tips to help you in this book.

45 – 60 Secretly super

Well done – you have great self-esteem. You know there's nothing wrong with feeling good about yourself and you won't let other people define you! This book will still give you some useful hints to help you get the most out of life.

Spend time finding out who you are. This means focusing on what you really like, not what you feel you should like, and working out what makes you happy in life and what doesn't. Forget about fitting in with friends and being cool – girls in the know work out what they're about and stick to it.

So What is Self-Esteem?

Self-esteem is about how much you value yourself and how important you think you are. It's not about being big-headed (that very loud girl who seems so confident is probably quite scared on the inside). It's simply about how you choose to rate yourself.

It's about knowing you're a good person, not worrying about being perfect, and believing you're as worthy as anyone else out there. It's important in life because it's the basis of your confidence and it powers the way you choose to live your life. Get good self-esteem and you'll have:

- confidence to try new and scary things
- a strong belief in yourself so that when things go wrong you don't crumble
- the ability to make good choices about your health and body
- the knack of keeping your problems in perspective
- lots of respect for who you are, even if it's different from everyone else
- a strong belief that you're a great person who deserves good things.

But if you've got low self-esteem, this could be you:

- you don't like yourself
- you put yourself down all the time
- you can't imagine why anyone would ever fancy you
- you worry your friends won't like you if you don't agree with them
- you feel lonely even in a crowd
- you hate yourself every day

you feel no one understands or knows the real you

 you feel you can't be yourself even with friends and family

 you secretly wish you were someone else

 you think you have nothing to offer the world.

'I want to think I can do something, but whenever I try something new, I hear a voice in my head saying, "You're rubbish – what makes you think you can do that?"'

Katie

So what happens to change us from cute babies without a care in the world to people who hate ourselves and our bodies? Well, it all comes down to what we believe about ourselves. For example: *I'm pretty. I'm shy. I'm rubbish at school. I'm ugly. I'm clumsy.*

These beliefs aren't just made up in our heads but are often based on what we experience in life – the things we're told about ourselves by friends, our families, teachers and sometimes our enemies.

Things like:
You have a bad temper. You're rubbish at sports. You're selfish. You're not as pretty as your sister.

The problem is that often these labels are not true, but they stick like glue and are hard to peel off. They eat away at our confidence and have us believing the worst about ourselves. But the truth is that people say things for all kinds of reasons – for a joke, or because they're in a bad mood, or because they are really talking about themselves. Sometimes they're even trying to be nice: *You're the clever one, aren't you?*

The way to bust the beliefs other people push on you is to question every label someone throws your way. Ask yourself: is what they're saying really true? If it's not true, you can tell them straight away that they're wrong. If you're not feeling quite that brave, you can still just decide inside that they're wrong and you won't take any notice of what they're saying. Remember:

1. You know yourself better than anyone else does.
2. You have the right to say, 'No, you're wrong about that'.

3. You can come up with a new belief / label about yourself any time you want.
4. You don't have to believe what others say about you.
5. Just because you aren't good at one thing doesn't mean you're rubbish at everything.

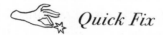 *Quick Fix*

Think of a label someone has tried to stick on you. Did you believe them? Was the label true? If not, replace it with your own new label, which describes the real you.

It's a good idea to have a special notebook to write down your ideas, so you can keep track of what you're aiming for, and how you're making your life more fabulous!

THE GIRLS IN THE KNOW SELF-ESTEEM RULES

Ask yourself these questions: Am I being too mean to myself? Am I being my own worst enemy? If the answer is yes, decide RIGHT NOW that from today you're going to be your own best friend.

You can start by following the Girls in the Know Self-Esteem Rules.

Rule One – Remember the good stuff!

Stop focusing on the bad stuff and start noticing all the good things about yourself. This can be anything from being kind to having a brilliant sense of humour, from being great at school work to having excellent taste in music.

To get you started, write down a list of twenty good things about yourself. For example:

* I'm funny.
* I'm a nice person.
* I'm good in a crisis.
* I have a lot of interests.
* I'm good at being silly.
* I help out at home.
* I am good fun.
* I'm a good listener.
* I make friends laugh with my emails and texts.
* I have great hair.
* I have lovely skin.
* I can do a handstand.
* I am tidy.

❀ I am good at art.

❀ I am happy with my own company.

❀ I have good taste in music.

❀ I always see the good in others.

❀ I am not mean.

❀ I am a good shoulder to cry on.

❀ I am positive.

Every time something gets you down, or you feel useless or unattractive, reel off three things from your list:

- one trait to remind yourself you're a good person.

- one trait to remind yourself you're as worthy as anyone else.

- one trait to remind yourself you deserve to be happy.

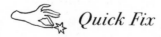 *Quick Fix*

If you can't think of twenty good things about yourself, ask your best friend or your mum to help you. Sometimes other people are much better at spotting our great traits than we are.

Rule Two – Silence your negative voice

This is about how you speak to yourself. We all have a nasty little voice inside our heads which puts us down, tells us we can't do things and laughs at us when we want to try something new. It might be saying, 'There's no way you'll be picked for the team', or maybe, 'You'll make a fool of yourself if you join the drama group', or, 'You don't seriously think you're thin enough to wear that skirt?'. This voice is actually your mind's safety mechanism, which is there to stop you doing anything which might end in failure or embarrassment.

The trouble is, if you listen too hard to this little voice, you'll be cutting yourself off from all kinds of experiences which could make you feel great and grow stronger. People with truly fabulous lives are the ones who risk trying new things. If they don't succeed every time, so what? They try something else!

So the next time you're about to do something and a voice pops into your head saying, 'Don't be silly

– you can't do that / be that / try that' – turn round and ask 'Why not?'

Watch out, though: questioning your voice can make it get even louder, and you might find that more and more scary scenarios start running through your head. But don't give in to it! Keep asking, 'Why not?' until the voice gets quieter and quieter and you find the courage to go for whatever you want. Remember, courage isn't about feeling brave, but about being brave when you feel scared.

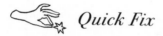 *Quick Fix*

Think of a time recently when your negative voice stopped you doing something you wanted to do. Try challenging it and see what happens. Maybe it's not too late!

Rule Three – Be whoever you want to be

This means being who YOU want to be, not who others say you are, or who your teachers think you can be, or who your parents would like you to be. These people may all want the best for you, but to feel happy you need to be true to yourself. That's not about trying to fit in with the crowd, and definitely not being what others want you to be so they like you.

It can be hard to stand up and say, 'THIS IS WHO I AM' when you're an adult, never mind when you're young. But don't panic: your decision to be yourself doesn't have to be as open as this. You can make it a secret decision and start living it in small ways day by day. For instance, if a friend's gossip about other people gets you down, decide you won't join in. You don't have to slate her for doing it, just refuse to get drawn in. Or, say you want to change your look, you don't have to tell the world – just start choosing clothes which are closer to your ideal, and see if you can have a different haircut.

Finally, remember you can change who you are and who you want to be at any time in your life. So what if last year you were the Queen of Nasty, or Little Miss Frightened, or the Rebel Girl? This year you can be whoever you want to be!

Quick Fix

Have you said or done something recently just to fit in with your friends? Decide not to do the same thing again and to be true to yourself instead. Write down your decision. For example, *I won't join in when Chloe starts being horrible about Daisy* – and write down what happens.

Top Ten Secrets of Self-Esteem

1. Don't let others decide who you are.
2. Say something good to yourself five times a day.
3. When in doubt, talk about your successes, not your failures.
4. Learn from your mistakes, don't let them get you down.
5. Be body positive – look at yourself positively not critically.
6. To feel confident, think posture and breathing. Stand upright, breathe deeply and think, 'World, here I come'.
7. Remember everyone's as scared as you.

8. It doesn't matter if you say or do something embarrassing.
9. When you feel nervous, think outwards not inwards – focus on what other people are doing and how they might be feeling.
10. Keep telling yourself you're as good as anyone else.

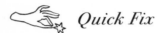 *Quick Fix*

If there are things about yourself that you want to change, make goals for yourself. For example, if you want to be nicer, give out three compliments a day. Then see what happens. Does the new way you're behaving make other people respond differently to you?

What is Body Image?

Body image is how you feel about your body and your looks. It's linked to self-esteem because it's all about how you see yourself and how you think other people see you. Up until recently you may have happily gone through life without even thinking much about your looks beyond: *Do I like what I am wearing?* and *Does my hair look OK?*. What changes all this is puberty, when your body goes through some pretty radical changes that may freak you out.

These changes mean you may start comparing yourself to others, thinking: *Am I good enough?* or *Why aren't I pretty like her?* or *Why aren't I as tall as her?*

This kind of thinking doesn't get you anywhere. Everyone is different, and the important thing is to learn to accept yourself as you are. So, let's find out how good (or bad) your body image is.

Your Secret Self Quiz 2

How Do You Feel About Your Body?

1. When you think of your body you wish:
   a. you looked like someone else   (5)
   b. you had enough money for plastic surgery   (10)
   c. you could get fitter   (0)

2. When you enter a party the first thing you do is:
   a. look for good-looking boys   (0)
   b. work out who's fatter than you   (10)
   c. look for a plant to hide behind   (5)

3. When you walk past shop windows you always:
   a. check out how fat your behind looks   (5)
   b. avoid your reflection at all costs   (10)
   c. look to see how good you look   (0)

4. On holiday you'd never be seen dead without:
    a. a sarong   (5)
    b. a bikini   (0)
    c. a big, baggy T-shirt   (10)

5. You read celebrity magazines:
    a. to see famous people's flaws up close   (5)
    b. to motivate yourself to lose weight   (10)
    c. for a laugh   (0)

6. If a boy you liked said you needed to lose weight,
    what would you do?
    a. do it   (10)
    b. tell him to get a face lift and forget about him (0)
    c. tell him to get lost, but cry yourself to sleep   (5)

Now total your scores.

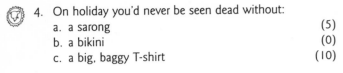

0 – 5 Healthy balance

Well done, you have a healthy view of your body and
a good balance of what to worry about and what to
ignore. Keep reading for handy hints on getting fit and
beating those body blips.

10 – 15 Halfway there

Careful – you are about to cross the line between what's normal to worry about and what's OTT. Keep reading to find out how to stop worrying and start getting more out of life.

20 – 30 The only way is up

You've let your fears about how you look stop you from seeing who you really are, and it's getting you down. Talk to someone you trust about how you're feeling, and keep reading to find out how to feel better about yourself.

Try not to bottle up your body worries. You may feel embarrassed about them, but confiding in someone you trust - maybe your mum or your best friend - can really help you get things in perspective.

THE GIRLS IN THE KNOW BODY IMAGE RULES

To help you accept yourself as you are, follow the Girls in the Know Body Image Rules.

Rule One – Don't be celebrity obsessed

This is a MAJOR rule, because we now live in a world obsessed with how famous people look. Think of all the newspapers, magazines and TV shows obsessed with how thin or fat famous people are, how good (or bad) their skin looks, how lumpy they are under their clothes, or how they've 'let themselves go', or how they've improved their looks via surgery.

Getting hooked into this kind of celebrity culture does two really bad things:

1. It makes you overly critical about your own body.
2. It gives you the idea that in order to be beautiful you have to be perfect.

The reality is there is no such thing as perfect, and if you start taking too much notice of celebrities' bodies you're putting yourself on a road to misery. Celebrity mags can be good for a laugh, but make sure you don't take them seriously.

 *Quick Fix*

Find an old magazine or newspaper with pictures of celebrities showing how fat /thin /spotty they are. Do you think these pictures help you feel good about yourself? If not, tear them up into tiny pieces and throw them away!

'I stopped reading all those celebrity magazines because all they do is point out what's wrong with everyone's bodies all the time. They're always saying, "She's too fat, he's got a belly, she's got hair under her arms". It made me really critical about my own body and everyone else's.'

Lucy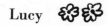

Rule Two – Be nice about other people

Putting other people down and being negative about their looks is a sign you don't like your own body. If you felt confident about yourself you wouldn't feel the need to slate others. If you want to boost your body image, start by viewing other people positively. This means focusing on the good things about everyone's bodies. This is a brilliant thing to do because it shows that people don't have to be perfect to be attractive. Once you start accepting the differences in other people's shapes, sizes and looks, you'll find it easier to be more forgiving towards your own body.

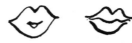

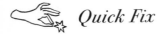 *Quick Fix*

Next time you're out shopping, or in a bus queue, spend a minute watching all the people who go by. Choose one thing you like about how they look. It might be incredible eyes, or a great curvy figure, or a dazzling smile. See how different everyone is, and how people who are happy with their bodies look fabulous, even if they don't have perfect skin or a perfect figure.

Rule Three – Give yourself a break!

Don't let worries about your body rule your life
and bring you down. It's a waste of time, because
you'll never have the perfect body – nobody does –
even if you had plastic surgery, were the ideal
weight and exercised non-stop! So give yourself a
break and, instead of obsessing about what you
haven't got, focus on what's good about your
body.

Above all, remember that wishing you were
someone else means you're wishing everything
about yourself away. You are who you are, and
that's someone very special – even if you haven't
quite realised that yet. If you want to be a Girl in
the Know, learn to appreciate yourself! It's tiring
being so down on yourself all the time – don't
you deserve some fun like everyone else?

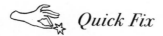 *Quick Fix*

Write down ten things you like about your
body. This might be your shiny hair, your
good skin, nice fingernails or elegant
ankles – or how strong or agile you are.

Set yourself a challenge and make it something you've previously been scared of. It might be trying a new sport or activity, wearing a different style, or maybe speaking up in class. Meeting a challenge is a great self-esteem booster!

CHAPTER 2

Getting into Shape

'I hate it when I say I'm fat and my family say I'm not. I know they're lying because I can see I'm bigger than all my friends. Why do people just tell me what they think I want to hear? It makes me think I can't trust anyone.'

Kelly

Do you think a lot about your weight? Being fat is the number one body worry for most girls. It's not surprising – being surrounded by pictures of skinny celebrities is enough to make anyone feel enormous. And you can hardly turn on the TV without hearing someone going on about how young people are too fat or too thin.

But if you're thinking of going on a diet, STOP! There's something very important you need to know.

DIETS DON'T WORK.

Why not? Because a diet makes you stick to a rigid eating plan. It might work for a while, and you might find that you lose a bit of weight – but then you get sick of having to keep to the rules. You start craving all the foods you're not allowed, and you end up slipping back into the kind of bad eating habits that made you want to diet in the first place. If you've never tried dieting yourself, you've probably seen your mum, your sister or a friend go through this.

Whatever you weigh, the secret of feeling good about your weight is very, very simple:

1. Eat healthily.
2. Do more exercise.

That's all there is to it. Easier said than done? Read on to find out how.

Eat Yourself Gorgeous

Unlike dieting, healthy eating is a plan for life. Learn to eat healthily and you'll easily reach your ideal weight and stay there. Even better, you'll never have to think about going on a diet. Healthy eating is:

❀ eating a variety of foods every day

❀ eating fruit and vegetables every day

❀ eating wholegrains (such as wholemeal bread, brown rice and wholewheat pasta)

❀ eating more protein (such as lean meats and fish)

- eating raw foods and foods in their natural state
- eating because you're hungry and stopping when you're not.

It's also:

- eating fewer sugary foods (such as cakes, biscuits and sweets)
- eating fewer fatty foods (such as crisps or chips)
- knocking the fast-food and ready-meals habit on the head
- swapping fizzy drinks for water.

 Quick Fix

Have you just read the lists above and thought 'yuck'? The chances are you've never given healthy eating a try. Change your mindset by challenging yourself to eat one new, healthy food every day this week.

Healthy food is simply good food that's close to its natural state. So it's the food you already eat – but before it's been messed with! It could be the strawberries you usually have in ice cream or milk shakes, the chicken breast or steak that you usually order as a burger from a fast-food place, or the vegetables you usually have on a pizza. The only difference is that these foods haven't been swamped in fat, sugar and salt and so are still healthy!

So step one to getting in shape and feeling good about your body is to stop being a baby about food. Give healthy food a try before you knock it. If you can consider a diet that allows you to have nothing but soup all week or forces you to skip two meals a day, it's got to be easier to try a healthy approach that lets you eat everything, but in a different way!

Step two is to get your mum (or whoever does the shopping and cooking at home) on side. Explain why you want to eat more healthily – for example, to get fit or feel better about yourself – so she can see that this is not just a fad diet. Emphasise that you want to eat more fruit and vegetables and less processed food. Try promising to help with the shopping and cooking too – this can help persuade even the most reluctant mum that your new eating habits won't make her busy life even busier! Better still, offer to make up your own lunch box, so your mum can cross one task off her list completely.

'Vegetables and fruit – no way! I'd rather be fat than eat that!'

Claire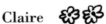

Eat in a healthy way and:

- ❀ it will help you lose weight if you need to
- ❀ it will give you more energy
- ❀ it will keep you happy
- ❀ it will help you feel good about yourself
- ❀ it will make you feel healthy
- ❀ it will put you off dieting for life

❀ it will give you a taste for new foods

❀ it will help you sleep better

❀ it will make your skin glow.

To find your true shape, look at your family. For example, if everyone in your family is short and oval-shaped, then the chances are that you're never going to be long and leggy – but you can still be slim and healthy.

PUBERTY AND YOUR WEIGHT

A quick word about puberty. This is the process of change from childhood to adulthood which starts between the ages of eight and thirteen. You're used to getting taller as you get older, but puberty makes you grow outwards as well as upwards. This can be a bit of a shock! Even if you've been a beanpole all your life, or someone who has always been able to eat and eat without gaining weight, you might suddenly find you change shape quite quickly. Your breasts will grow and your hips and tummy may get more curvy. You might find your jeans get tight almost overnight, or that stretch marks (see page 70) appear. Adults may make annoying comments like, 'Goodness – haven't you grown?'

This extra bulk can be frustrating, but you have to learn to relax about it. Your body needs to lay down fat in order to kickstart the important changes of puberty, such as the start of your periods. It's a really bad idea to try to stop this weight gain by dieting or overdoing the exercise.

When you feel bad about your body, remind yourself that you're still going through puberty. Your moods and your body are being affected and you're not yet looking at the end result!

WHAT TO DO IF YOU REALLY THINK YOU'RE OVERWEIGHT

It can be really hard to know if you're overweight, obese (seriously overweight), or just imagining you're fat when you're not. A good rule of thumb is to go by how you feel and what people say to you. Ask yourself these questions:

1. Can you run for a bus without nearly passing out?
2. Can you easily get clothes to fit you?
3. Do people tell you you're being silly when you say you're worried about your weight?
4. Does your body feel strong and fit?
5. Do close friends and family drop hints about the benefits of healthy eating and exercise in front of you?

If you've answered no to questions one to four and yes to question five, it's possible that you are overweight. To find out for sure, see your doctor and ask his/her advice. Your doctor will weigh you (in confidence), talk to you about what you're eating and then tell you if you need to lose weight, how much to lose and how to lose it. If you are told you're 'overweight' or 'obese', try not to get hung up on a label. What's more important is not what weight category you fall into right now, but what you decide to do about it from this moment on.

Everyone's weight can fluctuate by as much as three pounds (nearly one and a half kilos) a day. Around the time of your period, your body holds back more water, which has a big effect on your weight, and can make you feel bloated too. So don't torture yourself with regular weigh-ins – the only thing they'll do is have you reaching for comfort food or a faddy diet. The smart way to judge your weight is to go by the fit of your usual clothes – maybe your favourite pair of jeans.

Top Ten Weight Tips

1. Diets don't work – they just make you obsessed with the foods you can't have.
2. Everyone can lose weight if they need to.
3. Skipping meals and starving yourself is not healthy eating.
4. Allow yourself a little bit of what you like.
5. Forget the scales – go by how your clothes feel.
6. At every meal you should have a variety of colours on your plate. If your food is all shades of yellow and brown, you're missing out on some important vitamins and other goodies.
7. Check labels and steer clear of foods with a high proportion of fat, sugar and salt.
8. Don't be too strict with yourself.
9. Drink two litres of water a day – it will stop you reaching for fattening snacks.
10. Work out why you reach for food when you're not hungry (see next page).

Why We Eat

For most of us, eating is not just about satisfying hunger pangs. Sometimes we eat to fit in with our friends. Or we might eat because we're bored, or fed up and in need of some comfort. We can use food to spoil ourselves or even to punish ourselves. The question you need to ask yourself is – why do YOU eat?

Have you been munching on something as you read this? If so, you've probably not even been aware that you've been eating. You're not alone – most of us snack mindlessly while we do other things and so don't even realise how much food we get through in a day.

Try keeping a food diary for a week. List everything you eat, when you ate it and how you felt before and after eating. This will give you an idea of how much you eat and also why and when you eat. You might be really surprised at what you find! Your food diary entries will help you work out:

✱ **Your trigger points**

That's what time of the day you're more likely to reach for unhealthy foods or snacks to boost your energy and help you to feel less tired (usually about three or four p.m. in most people).

✱ **How your moods affect your eating patterns**

Does being upset make you eat more or less? Some people can't eat when they're upset, while others find they can't stop eating.

✱ **What foods you reach for**

You may think you're eating five portions of fruit and vegetables a day but perhaps you're really averaging two portions and five chocolate bars.

❀ **What foods act as a comfort**

What foods make you feel better? In most people these are sugar-based or fatty foods.

❀ **How food affects your body image**

How do you feel about yourself when you overeat? Some people feel bad, then get into a vicious cycle of eating, feeling bad about themselves and then eating even more.

Understanding why you eat is the first step to changing your habits for the better. If you know you tend to hit the chippy on the way home from school when you're tired and hungry, pack a banana to keep you going till you get home. Or if you always reach for the biscuit tin when you're feeling down, remind yourself that it just makes you feel worse, and grab an apple instead.

Girls in the Know

Who you are today doesn't determine who you'll be tomorrow, unless you keep doing the same things. You can change whenever you choose by starting to do something different.

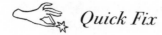 *Quick Fix*

Before you eat a snack, ask yourself:

- How hungry am I? (Give your hunger pangs a mark out of ten – if it's seven or under, don't eat!)
- How much do I want this chocolate bar over something healthier like fruit?
- If I waited ten minutes would I still want this?
- What do I want more – this snack or a fitter body?

WHAT TO EAT

If your aim is to get in shape, you have to be honest with yourself. A diet where you skip breakfast, scoff a packet of crisps on the bus or a Mars bar at eleven a.m. and eat a slice of pizza and chips for lunch is not healthy and won't help your weight, even if you're opting for low-fat crisps and pizza with vegetables. To eat healthily, follow the Girls in the Know Food Rules.

Rule One – Always eat breakfast

Surveys show that thirty per cent of people aged twelve to eighteen years skip breakfast every single day. That's bad news, as breakfast gives you vital energy for the day and nutrients that stop weight gain. Studies show that girls who avoid eating before school eat more fatty foods at lunch and break times and so gain weight compared to those who eat breakfast. If you're not used to eating first thing, start by drinking a glass of orange juice every day and then move on to toast or cereal (but not a sugar-coated one).

 *Quick Fix*

If you're always too rushed to stop for breakfast in the morning, get up ten minutes earlier. You'll lose ten minutes' sleep, but you'll have more energy later on.

Rule Two – Cut back on fast and processed foods

If you're a fast-food princess then it's likely you opt for these foods because:

1. They are cheap.
2. All your friends eat them.
3. They taste good.

The bad news is that fast food tastes good and is cheap because it's full of fat and sugar. Sadly if you're trying to get fit, you need to cut out fast and processed foods (prepared foods which you buy from the supermarket that are similar to fast food, such as ready meals and pies) because they will pack on weight. It's a tough one, especially if you crave burgers and pizza. However, bear in mind that your cravings will lessen after only a week if you make the switch to healthy food.

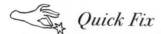 *Quick Fix*

See if you can get one or two friends to join your healthy eating campaign. It's a lot easier to ditch the junk food habit if you're not on your own!

Rule Three – Snack wisely

The foods you choose to snack on could all be secretly pumping up your body fat. While we all need two snacks a day between meals, you need to learn to snack wisely. Eat fruit instead of crisps and chocolate, or a pot of yogurt instead of biscuits.

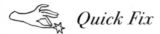 *Quick Fix*

Try to take a healthy snack with you when you go out, so you won't be tempted to buy sweet or fatty foods at the corner shop.

Rule Four – Eat a WIDE range of foods every day

This is the bit where you might start saying, 'But I hate X and Y and Z'. If you truly hate a particular food such as cheese or apples, that's fine. But if you say you hate all vegetables or fruit, it sounds as if you're not being brave enough to experiment and try new things. Give yourself at least three tries on something before you give up on it.

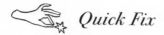 *Quick Fix*

Somewhere out there is a vegetable and a fruit you will like – it could just be that you're not eating it in the right way. So try it raw, cooked, and with something else added (but not something fatty like cheese or chocolate sauce – try plain yogurt).

Rule Five – Have a little of what you like

This is healthy eating, not diet denial, so a little of what you like will stop you craving it. You could allow yourself one small chocolate bar a day, or one fizzy drink a week, or one trip to the burger bar a week – but remember, the more treats you allow yourself the harder it will be to get in shape and stay in shape.

Rule Six – Read between the lines

Some foods are not as healthy as they sound.

❋ **Lite/Light**
These labels often mean nothing and lead you to believe a food is healthy, but really it could simply mean the texture of the product is whipped to taste lighter.

❋ **No added sugar**
This doesn't mean what you're eating is sugar free, but that no sugar has been added to the existing content. It could still be packed with sugar.

❋ **Low fat**
The fat content is low, but it may not be fat free or low in calories (it may still be high in sugar).

❋ **Fresh juice**
Legally, all drinks can use the words 'fresh' and 'juice' even if they contain as little as one per cent pure juice, so stick to the real, pure one hundred per cent juice.

 *Quick Fix*

One way to avoid hidden fats, sugars, and extra calories is to know what's in your food. So get to know your way round a food label. Ingredients are listed with the greatest amount first. So if sugar, butter and salt are listed first, you know the product's not healthy!

Rule Seven – Zap the fizzy drinks

Fizzy drinks are often loaded with sugar (sometimes up to thirteen teaspoons per can!) but opting for a diet version is no better for your health. It may be sugar free but it's what's known as nutritionally empty – that means it doesn't give your body anything useful. Many diet drinks also contain caffeine, a substance which can make you irritable and anxious. A can of diet cola, for instance, contains approximately forty-five mg of caffeine (that's as much as a small cup of coffee). If you're craving the fizz, opt for sparkling water and flavour it with a piece of lemon or lime. (But watch out for some flavoured bottled waters – they can be packed with sugars and syrups.)

Rule Eight – Portion control

If you think you're eating healthily, but you're still gaining a lot of weight, or everyone is telling you that you're losing too much weight, it's likely you're getting your portion control wrong.

Knowing how much to eat is as important as knowing what to eat – and it's something a lot of people get wrong. Studies show that the average meal portion size has gone up three times since the 1970s – which is just part of the reason why as a nation we've got fatter.

These are the standard portion sizes you should stick to:

* A portion of meat is about the size of an adult's palm
* A portion of hard cheese is the size of a matchbox
* A portion of potatoes, rice or pasta should be the size of a tennis ball.

Avoid anything super-sized or labelled something like 'twenty-five per cent extra'. If you're treating yourself to crisps, make sure you have a normal bag, not a 'big eat', and ask your mum to buy packs of individual bags, rather than a large bag you'll be tempted to sneak into all the time!

Drink more water! A glass of water every half an hour will stop you feeling hungry and tired and help your skin look amazing.

 *Quick Fix*

If you hate drinking plain water then start by diluting fruit juices – half water, half juice. You'll soon get used to drinking more water and a less sweet taste.

'When my mum needed to lose weight, we all decided to help her – so my brother and I stopped eating takeaways and asking for chocolate, and we ate the same meals as her. It was great – we all ended up losing weight and feeling better.'

Lisa

Fit and Fabulous

We all have parts of our body we hate – perhaps it's a tummy that concertinas when you sit down, or thighs that wobble when you walk.

We've already looked at healthy eating. The second way to get the body of your dreams is to start moving your butt! The good news is you don't have to be amazing at sport. You can get fit even if you're no good at running, or if you're the kind of girl who's always picked last for teams. The trick is to put in maximum effort every time you do something, to find an activity that you like and to work on being active all the time – even when you're at home relaxing. Get the combination right and exercise will:

※ keep you healthy on the inside (it's good for your heart)
※ stop you getting overweight
※ make you look trim and slim (as it's exercise that knocks off the centimetres)
※ improve your mood
※ improve your skin and hair
※ boost your self-esteem
※ make you feel as if you can achieve anything!

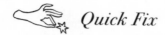 *Quick Fix*

Remember to eat healthily every day as well as exercising – you have to do both together to get results.

So what's your excuse for not exercising?

✸ I have no willpower or time

If you can queue for hours for the new Harry Potter book, or painstakingly download games from the Net, or watch DVDs, you have willpower and time to get fit! To dig into your inner power, decide on a definite goal – for example to lose weight / boost your confidence / fit into your new jeans.

✸ It's not cool

Tell that to Wayne Rooney, David Beckham and Maria Sharapova! Find a sport or activity that suits your personality and you'll be too busy enjoying it to worry about what the other slackers say.

❀ I'm not sporty

If PE turns you off, then search for the activity that gets you personally fired up and going – dancing, walking to the shops every day, mountain-biking, skating – it all counts as exercise.

❀ My friends will think I'm weird

They won't think you're odd once you start getting in shape and running rings around them. Better still, rope them in, as studies show that getting an exercise buddy helps keep you motivated, increases your staying power and makes it more fun.

THE RIGHT EXERCISE FOR YOU

Exercise is not just the stuff you do in PE or the matches you watch on TV. One of these is bound to fit into your life.

Power-walking

How to do it: Simply walk but, instead of strolling, walk as briskly as you can, pumping your arms up and down as you go. To make it harder, power-walk up and down hills as it takes more effort and so your legs and bottom and heart have to work harder.

Benefits: Power-walking tones your thighs, calves, bottom and stomach. It also burns calories and fat, and increases your stamina.

Dancing

How to do it: It doesn't matter whether you're dancing around your room, or having a great night out. The key is to keep dancing continuously for as long as you can.

Benefits: Apart from the benefits to your heart and lungs, dancing makes you more flexible and stronger, and improves your balance. Better still the movements can help tone and strengthen parts of the leg, stomach and back.

Swimming

How to do it: Don't race, instead make sure you take slow, full strokes and swim continuously (hanging around the pool edges doesn't count).

Benefits: Swimming is a fantastic workout for the whole body as it ensures you use both your upper body and lower body and increases your overall fitness.

Cycling

How to do it: Cycle at a steady pace, focusing on how you're using your legs, and now and then challenge yourself with some small hills.

Benefits: Cycling works the arms and legs. If you want to work your lower body and bottom keep your seat low; alternatively keep the seat high and lean forwards to work the upper body.

Walking

How to do it: Just put one foot in front of the other as you go shopping with your mates, walk to school or explore somewhere new. To get the right benefit, walk for at least thirty minutes at a vigorous pace – you should be able to still hold a conversation, but at the end you'll feel tired.

Benefits: Walking is healthier than you might think. It tones all the muscles in your body, increases stamina, and helps you to feel fitter and healthier, especially if you're outside breathing in lots of lovely fresh air.

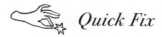 *Quick Fix*

See how much progress you're making by noticing what happens when you do everyday activities. Can you run up the stairs without gasping for breath, or run for the bus without passing out? You'll be amazed how quickly things improve as you get fitter.

'Friends used to laugh when I said I was going to get into exercise. Now I'm slimmer and fitter than all of them, and on the swimming team, so they're not laughing any more.'

Hannah

How Much Exercise?

The recommendation is that all under-eighteens should get sixty minutes of exercise a day. It sounds a lot, but don't despair: this can be done in ten-minute segments throughout the day and can include all kinds of non-sporty things like walking to and from school, walking the dog, and even going out dancing with your mates.

Here are two examples of how you might clock up your hour-a-day of exercise:

On a school day
A brisk fifteen-minute walk to a friend's house / school / shops and back = thirty minutes,

PLUS
A PE lesson where you actually move = thirty minutes.

At the weekend
Ten minutes' dancing in your room (without stopping),

PLUS
Twenty minutes' cycle ride.

PLUS
Thirty minutes' swimming.

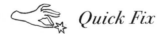 *Quick Fix*

Choose to be active whenever you can. Just getting up to turn the TV over, running upstairs for your mum, or getting off the bus one stop earlier will help you get fit.

Your Secret Self Quiz 3

How Sporty Are You?

1. You don't like exercise because:
   a. you feel too fat / too rubbish for it (0)
   b. it's too much effort (5)
   c. well . . . actually, you don't mind it (10)

2. When it comes to being picked for teams:
   a. you're always the first to be picked (10)
   b. you're always the last to be picked (0)
   c. you don't care if you're picked or not (5)

3. You secretly wish:
   a. you were good at sports (0)
   b. you never had to exercise again (5)
   c. you could be a sports star (10)

4. When you're at home:
   a. you exercise more than at school (10)
   b. you exercise less than at school (5)
   c. you do no exercise (0)

Now total your scores.

0 – 10 Sports shy

You say you hate sports, but secretly you're lacking in confidence and feel embarrassed about your abilities. We're not all made to be sports stars, so work on finding an activity (see pages 50–52) that suits you best and use that as your main source of exercise.

15 – 25 Sports lazy

Laziness is the reason why you veer away from sport and activity. You can always find a hundred things you'd rather be doing. To start seeing the benefits of being active, choose something that fires your imagination. Think less about team sports and more about individual or extreme ones.

30 – 40 Sports savvy

You like sports and being active, but may be surrounded by those who ridicule it. Be your own person and excel where you want to excel.

CHAPTER 3

Zit Attacks, Nasty Niffs and Bad Hair Days

❀❀

'Why do adults always come up to you and say, "You've got a huge spot on the end of your nose", or "Your hair needs a wash"? Don't they remember what puberty is like?'

Sam ❀❀

Broken nails, bad hair days and skin that goes bump in the night? We all have days when we wake up, look in the mirror and feel like screaming. So here's a trouble-shooting guide to the world of beauty blips, focusing on what works and what doesn't.

Your Skin

Having great skin makes you feel fantastic. Look after it by:

* Eating well – good skin needs a good diet with lots of vitamins and minerals. Keep reading for more about this.

* Not blasting it with sun – just because your skin is young and strong doesn't mean it can take a roasting. More on this later too.

* Drinking lots of water – the skin is a living organ and in order to look glowing and fresh and bright it needs water to hydrate it.

* Getting your beauty sleep – eight hours a night at least, if you want to look good!

Spot SOS

You may be spot free right now, with a complexion a supermodel would be jealous of, but sooner or later spots rear their ugly heads in most girls' lives. Having spots is a guaranteed way to make even the most confident person feel unattractive and self-conscious. The good news is that if you understand your spots, why you get them and how to blast them, you won't have to go through your teenage years hiding your face under a fringe and masses of make-up.

Firstly, it's worth knowing that it's not just you: ninety-nine per cent of teenagers will get spots, and eighty per cent will get acne, and it's all down to puberty. Acne is the medical name for when you keep getting more than one spot, and it's caused when the skin's sebaceous glands start producing more oil during puberty. The oil helps keep skin moist and supple, but it can block up the skin's pores, which become infected and turn into spots.

Acne tends to appear on your face, chest and back, because this is where the sebaceous glands are mainly found (though not everyone gets acne on their chests and backs). Whiteheads and blackheads are different kinds of spots which usually appear around the nose, forehead and chin, and occur when there is a blockage of the hair follicles rather than a normal skin pore.

Zap those zits

These days no one expects you to just suffer with spots, and there are some great treatments to help you get rid of them.

I. Look for products with Benzoyl Peroxide

While any products offering a miracle cure should be avoided, those with Benzoyl Peroxide can help moderate acne. This chemical not only helps reduce bacteria on the skin but also acts as a peeling agent to help loosen blackheads. The downside is Benzoyl Peroxide can make your skin go red and flaky because it is quite strong. Read the label carefully and follow the instructions.

2. Look for products with Azelaic Acid

This works in similar ways to Benzoyl Peroxide.

3. See your doctor

If nothing you buy over the counter helps, see your doctor and ask for antibiotics – the main ones are tetracycline and doxycycline. They will blast your spots, but be aware they can take up to six months to work.

Your spot may look as big as China but it is probably nowhere near as huge as you imagine. This is because peering at your face two centimetres away from a mirror will always make your blemishes seem bigger.

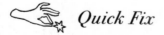 *Quick Fix*

How to camouflage your spot: Start by choosing a make-up concealer which matches your skin colour. Apply it with a brush and then gently brush loose foundation powder over it to seal the concealer. You're ready to go!

GIRLS IN THE KNOW GUIDE TO PICKING YOUR SPOTS

In an ideal world none of us would pick spots, but in reality there's nothing like waking up and being faced with a corker to make you lose all sense and reason. It's best not to squeeze, but if you're going to, make sure you squeeze sensibly. This means:

- Don't touch red, hard and painful spots. These are deep, infected spots and will hurt and just become more inflamed (think HUGE) if you attack them. These spots are just un-squeezable!

- Never squeeze with your fingernails, as this scars the skin. Use two tissues and the sides of your fingers, and don't squeeze inwards but pull the skin apart to let the spot 'pop' out.

- Let the spot dry for at least an hour if you are going to apply make-up on top. Try dabbing something with anti-bacterial qualities (like tea tree oil) on it first.

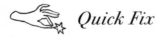 *Quick Fix*

If you really *must* squeeze, always wash your hands and nails with soap first to avoid spreading more spots across your face.

Top Ten Spot Tip-Offs

1. Spots aren't always caused by particular foods like chocolate or chips.
2. Spots don't mean you're dirty.
3. Picking your spots will make them spread.
4. Your doctor can give you something for your spots.
5. Acne is the name given to recurring spots.
6. Most people grow out of spots when puberty ends.
7. Spots get worse around your period when hormones fluctuate.
8. Dabbing on toothpaste doesn't zap spots.

9. Squeezing spots can make them larger.
10. You can't 'catch' spots from someone else.

THE SECRETS OF GLOWING SKIN

For fantastic, glowing skin you don't need to spend a fortune at the make-up counter. The secret is to feed your face properly, and to look after your skin in the right way. Here's how:

Eat for beauty

Chips and chocolate don't cause acne, but if you want fabulous skin, you do need to eat well. A healthy diet is your skin's best friend. This is because certain vitamins found in food stimulate the skin and help it to create new skin cells. For example:

Vitamin A, found in carrots, oily fish such as salmon, trout, sardines and mackerel, cheese, milk, spinach and eggs.

Vitamin C, found in green leafy vegetables such as broccoli and cabbage, and fruit such as strawberries, mangoes and oranges.

Vitamin E, found in avocados, eggs, nuts and seeds, wholemeal bread and wholewheat pasta.

And don't forget to drink loads of water!

'Drink more water for good skin? You've got to be joking. I love fizzy drinks, and water is so tasteless.'

Nell

Treat your skin kindly

Don't be suckered by beauty jargon or what you read in magazines. You don't need night creams, day creams, anti-ageing creams, toners, cleansers and exfoliators for good skin. All you need to do is wash your face every day and apply sun protection cream (see over the page).

Tempting as it is to attack your face with a scrubbing brush and one of those gritty face cleaners, be aware that your skin is delicate. Use mild products (unperfumed is best) to wash your face, and apply them gently – rubbing your skin vigorously in the hope that you'll blitz spots is like attacking a piece of glass with a wire brush! Gently does it if you want your skin to glow and look smooth. Don't use an exfoliator more than once a week, and pat your face dry with a soft, clean towel.

If you wear make-up, make sure you use the right colour, and don't overdo it. There's nothing more likely to make your skin look bad than too much make-up of the wrong colour. Choose foundation and concealers carefully (test them on your cheek and then view it in daylight, not under shop lights) and apply lightly so that you can hardly tell that it's there.

And remember to remove your make-up at night. Sleeping in make-up won't do any serious harm, but it will make your skin look lifeless in the morning – and ruin your bed sheets.

Use your sun sense

Sun-worshipping is very bad for your skin at any age, but especially when you're young. Most of the long-term skin damage done by the sun happens before you're eighteen. To avoid premature wrinkles and skin cancer, always follow these rules:

Avoid going out in the sun between eleven a.m. and three p.m., when the sun is at its hottest – if you're outside at this time, stay in the shade as much as you can. Cover up with a T-shirt, but remember that you can still burn through thin fabrics and wet clothes. (A hat and sunglasses are a good idea too.)

Use a sun cream with SPF fifteen or more (SPF means Sun Protection Factor). This will reduce the amount of burning rays that get into your skin. If you have fair or freckly skin, use a higher SPF. They go up to SPF fifty or more!

'My mum was born in Australia, so she's always slapped suncream and hats on us when we're out. I can't believe how burned some of my friends get, or how they think a tan makes you look healthy!'

Millie

Quick Fix

Make sun lotion part of your morning routine every day so you don't forget. Clean your teeth, wash your face, apply sunscreen and then go.

Everyone, no matter how young, needs to protect their skin in the sun.

No Sweat!

Sweating is natural – you can't stop it completely, no matter how much antiperspirant you spray on, or how many showers a day you take. It's normal to sweat under your arms, on your face, hands and feet and sometimes even on your back.

There's no need to freak out if you notice the odd smell now and again, or if your light perspiration sometimes turns into excessive sweatiness. Put it down to puberty again.

There are a few things you can do to limit the damage:

1. Make sure you shower every day, paying attention to your smelly bits.
2. Use an antiperspirant every morning.

3. Change into clean clothes every day. If you wash, but then put on the same clothes you wore yesterday, you will smell because your clothes will have yesterday's sweat on them.

4. Avoid clothes which make you sweatier. Artificial materials like nylon and Lycra don't absorb sweat, so you end up feeling and looking sweatier. Natural fibres like cotton or linen will help you keep your cool.

5. If you're really worried about smelling sweaty, carry wet wipes and a handbag-sized antiperspirant with you so you can have an emergency freshen-up session in the loo!

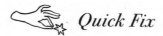 *Quick Fix*

If you really want to cut down your sweating, make sure you're using an antiperspirant, not a deodorant. The latter only masks smells with perfume, whereas an antiperspirant actually makes you sweat less.

Stretch Marks

Stretch marks happen to most people when they grow or gain weight really quickly (like during puberty or pregnancy). When this happens, the tissue under the skin is pulled by rapid growth. It may feel itchy and somewhat weird, and scars form rapidly. These are called stretch marks. At first, these may show up as reddish or purplish lines, but they turn lighter in time. Although there are creams that claim to eliminate stretch marks, the truth is they are useless, so don't waste your money. You can't make stretch marks go away, but don't worry, they will fade over time.

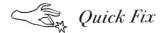 *Quick Fix*

If your stretch marks are itching, rub some body lotion into them to keep the skin supple and more flexible.

Bad Breath

Bad breath (halitosis) can be a major problem – especially if you're planning to kiss someone soon or whisper some gossip to your friend. It can happen if you don't clean your teeth regularly, and bacteria accumulate on the bits of food left in your mouth – yuck. Smoking and lack of water can also make this worse.

Contrary to popular belief, mouthwash or gum won't make bad breath go away. To make sure your mouth is really clean, floss, then brush your teeth for at least two minutes at least twice a day, See your dentist every six months for regular cleaning. If your breath is super bad, think about investing in a tongue scraper (available from chemists) – it's gross but it will clear your tongue of nasty-smelling bacteria. If none of this works, see your doctor.

If friends and family lean back when you talk to them, you may have bad breath that you don't know about. Don't be embarrassed – ask if you have, and then do something about it.

Healthy Hair

Aside from spots, periods and bad moods, puberty has another annoying effect on your body – it can change the look and feel of your hair. Even if you're someone who has never had to worry about having greasy or dry hair, you may suddenly find yourself having an extremely bad hair day – or a bad hair week, or month! Guess what? It's all down to those lovely hormones. We can't guarantee you'll never have a bad hair day again – everyone has the odd one – but with a few simple tricks you can make sure they hardly ever happen.

1. Load up on vitamins

For shiny, healthy hair, bolster your diet with foods rich in Vitamin A, such as cheese, eggs, milk, yogurt and oily fish such as salmon, trout, sardines and mackerel.

2. Don't wash your hair every day

Hair needs to be washed only every two to three days. Do it more often and you're washing out natural oils.

3. Treat your hair kindly

Tugging it, over-brushing it or playing with it when you're nervous will make your poor hair dirty and stressed. However, a two-minute rub down every day, massaging your scalp and gently pulling the hair, boosts circulation and promotes hair growth.

4. Go easy with the hairdryer

Blow-drying your hair takes out about a third of its natural moisture.

5. Be sparing with straightening

Hair-straighteners may make your hair look sleek, but ironing your hair can leave it dry and lifeless, so save them for special occasions.

6. Cut down on hair products

Too much serum, gel, mousse, wax or spray can overload your hair and leave it looking greasy and lank.

7. Drink more water

Dehydration can stop your hair growing, and make your hair dry and fragile – as well as making you feel drained and exhausted. Drink at least eight glasses of water a day.

8. If you have greasy hair

See if you can change your shampoo and conditioner for lighter products, and wash your hair less often. This is because frequent shampooing stimulates the oil glands in your scalp and makes your hair greasier.

9. If your hair is dry . . .

Invest in a good leave-in conditioner – that's one you don't have to wash out. Don't use too many products or treatments, and make sure you get your hair cut regularly.

10. If you have dandruff . . .

Don't panic. Switch to an anti-dandruff shampoo – this will make sure your shoulders stay flake-free.

How to Sail Through Your Periods

PMS (which stands for premenstrual syndrome) is the name for the lovely collection of symptoms that arrive up to ten days before your period. These can include mood swings, sugar cravings and bloating. Periods are a sign that your body is working properly – but that's not much comfort if you are feeling grumpy and huge! The good news is that most period problems can be zapped if you know what to do.

Gorging on sweet or salty food will just make you feel worse, so resist the temptation! Snack on fruit instead, and make sure you drink plenty of water and eat three proper meals a day.

You might feel like lounging on the sofa, but being active will make you feel better. To up your energy and banish the blues, make sure you do at least thirty minutes of exercise a day.

To feel good during your period, make sure you change your sanitary protection (aka pad or tampon) every three to four hours (or more if need be), and use the right size for your flow (see the packet for advice on this). Just shower once a day as usual – there's no need to get obsessed about hygiene or anxious about smells. Remember, you're experiencing something natural and normal, which all girls go through.

Just before your period, you can put on up to five pounds (about two and a quarter kilos) in weight. It can make you feel fat and bloated and your clothes may feel tight. But this isn't fat – it's fluid that will be lost during your period. So there's no need to go on a diet or give yourself a hard time. Just relax – it will all be gone in five days or so (just like your pre-period spots), and you'll be back to normal in no time.

Hair You Don't Want

As you go through puberty, you'll start to notice hair growing on different parts of your body – under your arms and around your private parts, as well as on your face and legs. If it bothers you, you can remove it. Hair on legs and underarms can be got rid of by shaving or waxing. Facial hair should never be shaved (as you'd end up with spiky stubble when it grew back), but it can be waxed, plucked or bleached.

If you think you are excessively hairy and feel embarrassed by it, do get yourself checked out by your doctor just to make sure that you don't have any hormonal problems. But make sure you don't get too hung up on getting rid of your body hair. It's natural, and it's much less obvious than you think. Let's face it, no one stares at your face or legs from two centimetres away like you do in front of a mirror! So don't start too early, as once you begin de-fuzzing, you need to keep doing it regularly.

To keep skin, hair and nails healthy make sure you eat plenty of zinc – it's found in seafood, walnuts, brazil nuts and sesame seeds, green vegetables, beef and wholegrain cereals.

Tip Top Nails

If you're in good health, your nails will be shiny and strong, with a smooth, pink surface.

The secrets of beautiful nails:

* Keep nails healthy by eating more dairy products (like milk or cheese), spinach, dried apricots, and oily fish (like sardines, mackerel and salmon) and seafood.

* Drink plenty of water.

* Keep nails strong by rubbing hand cream or oil into the base of the nail every day.

* Don't bite or nibble your nails – this makes them prone to flaking. Cut them instead.

❁ Avoid wear and tear by using rubber gloves when you wash up.

❁ Smooth out ridges on your nails using a nail buffer, available from chemists. Sometimes ridges run in families, or they can be caused if you catch your finger in the door, or something equally painful!

❁ If you have white spots on your nails, make sure you're eating a healthy diet including foods which contain zinc (see opposite). But they are often just caused by knocks and bangs – they grow out, so don't worry about them.

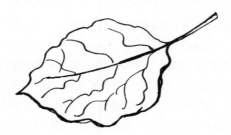

 *Quick Fix*

If you break a nail, don't bite or tear the broken bit off, or try to glue it back on. Just cut the broken piece off and then file gently straight across the nail to allow it to strengthen and grow again.

Top Ten Beauty Tips

1. Think about what goes into your body as well as what you put on your skin – both have an impact on your skin.

2. Always wear sunscreen in the summer, even on cloudy days.

3. Drink two litres of water a day to keep hydrated.

4. Don't waste your money on expensive creams – your skin is young and healthy, so it doesn't need much.

5. See your doctor if you keep getting spot attacks.

6. Get enough sleep – they call it beauty sleep for a reason. Aim for eight to ten hours a day.

7. Get active – it increases blood flow to the skin and so improves your skin.

8. Wash your make-up off – cleansed skin is healthy skin.

9. Don't over-scrub your face – this damages your skin.

10. To reduce the swelling on a spot, rub an ice cube on and around it.

CHAPTER 4

Horrible Habits and Health Foes

✿✿

'I do try to be healthy at home, but at school, junk's my thing. It's like stress relief – I always get a slice of pizza and chips with a cola and crisps for lunch. It can't be that bad, can it?'

Annie ✿✿

What horrible habits do you have? These are the secret things we indulge in that work against our health, our looks and our bodies.

Habits like eating crisps for breakfast and chocolate bars for lunch, sneaking the odd cigarette, and always expecting the worst. Some have huge repercussions for your future health; some just make you look and feel blobby. This chapter is about all those things you know you shouldn't do, but maybe choose to do anyway. Find out how to limit their impact, change your tune for the better and generally take responsibility for your own wellbeing!

Your Secret Self Quiz 4

Do You Need a Horrible Habit Overhaul?

1. Most of the time you feel:
   a. tired and blue   (10)
   b. excited and energetic (0)
   c. fed up and frustrated (5)

2. When you're bored you:
   a. eat junk food   (10)
   b. text a friend   (0)
   c. watch TV   (5)

3. Your worst habit is:
   a. biting your nails   (0)
   b. smoking   (10)
   c. overeating   (5)

4. Have you ever had a hangover?
   a. Never   (0)
   b. Once or twice   (5)
   c. Loads of times   (10)

5. Do you tend to:
   a. Expect the worst   (10)
   b. Hope things will be OK   (5)
   c. Expect everything to generally turn out well   (0)

Now total your scores.

0 – 15 Hardly horrible
You've got the healthy habit balance right – well done!
Read on to make sure you keep up the good work.

20 – 30 Halfway horrible
You may have one or two horrible habits – find out
how to kick them!

35 – 50 Horribly habits alert
You're threatening your health with some horrible
habits. This chapter shows you how to swap them for
healthy ones.

Horrible Habits

If you're lucky, you may not have a horrible health habit. If you do, it's not too late to give it up. If you don't, read on to find out what to avoid!

HORRIBLE HABIT ONE – SMOKING

Statistics show that one third of eleven-year-olds have experimented with smoking, and, by fifteen, around one in four teens are regular smokers, with girls more likely to smoke regularly than boys. It doesn't take a genius to know that smoking kills, but smoking also:

* gives you bad breath
* makes your teeth and fingers yellow
* dehydrates your skin so your skin gets more wrinkled and old-looking
* makes your periods more painful
* can cause depression
* can make you lacking in energy
* can put boys off kissing you.

Here's what else smoking will do for you.

✺ **It ruins your future fertility**

Having a baby may be the last thing on your
mind for the next fifteen to twenty years but
it's worth knowing that long-term smoking
could well stop you getting pregnant in the
future when you decide the time is right.
This is because cigarette smoke has been
shown to decrease fertility levels by as much
as fifty per cent.

✺ **It ups your risk of cancer**

Smoking causes one third of all cancer deaths
in the UK. To put this in perspective, you are
twenty-five times more likely to get lung cancer
if you smoke ten cigarettes or more a day.

✺ **It makes you snore LOUDLY**

Smoking irritates membranes in the nose and
throat and causes mucus to be secreted, and
turns up the snoring volume by causing tissues
in the nose to swell.

So why are you smoking?

Don't even say, 'It's the taste', because it can't be! If you're considering taking up smoking or smoke already, it's probably due to one of the following myths. Here's the truth behind all the smoke.

☼ **Myth: Smoking helps you to control your weight**
Studies show women who smoke are only one pound (about half a kilo) thinner than women who don't, which means smoking doesn't keep you thin at all.

☼ **Myth: It makes you feel sophisticated**
There's nothing sophisticated about bad breath, a smoker's cough, and yellow teeth and fingers.

☼ **Myth: It calms you down**
While smoking can make you feel sleepy, it's worth noting that it can also have a large stimulant effect – meaning that if you're stressed, all it will do is make you feel more anxious.

So don't even go there – smoking is a total waste of your money and your health. If you've already got the habit, decide TODAY that you're going to give up. For advice on how to do it, you can ring the NHS smoking helpline on 0800 169 0 169 or check out their website, www.givingupsmoking.co.uk.

To give up you have to do more than just cut down – you have to cut out all cigarettes in order to stop nicotine getting into your system and making you crave more.

'My sister smokes and it makes her smell. She's always chewing gum to take the smell away, but it's all over her clothes and in her hair. It puts me right off smoking.'

Mags

HORRIBLE HABIT TWO – DRINKING

The chances are that right now you don't drink,
though four per cent of eleven-year-olds and forty-
five per cent of fifteen-year-olds admit to drinking
ten units of alcohol a week (the equivalent of five
pints of ordinary strength lager or cider, or about
six glasses of wine, or about seven alcopops).

Alcohol is a horrible habit because it's a small step
from not drinking at all to drinking too much and
then relying on drink to get you through life. And,
contrary to popular belief, it doesn't just make
you relaxed and happy – all it does is take away
your usual judgement, lower your reaction time
and lead you into all kinds of accidents. If you
drink too much and on a regular basis:

❀ **It will make you fat**
Alcohol is full of empty calories because it's
basically made from sugar, which the body
stores as fat!

✺ It will make you cry
Alcohol is a depressant. It takes you to a nice rosy high for a short time and then brings you crashing back down to feelings of anxiety and depression.

✺ It makes you stupid
Any feelings of confidence are fleeting – then alcohol leads you to do reckless and stupid things you'd never do when sober.

✺ It will make you ill
A hangover makes you feel terrible and is a sign you have poisoned your body with alcohol.

✺ It will ruin your skin
Alcohol decreases the elasticity of the skin, causing it to age faster, become more wrinkled and basically make you look like an old hag.

'I used to drink to fit in with my friends. It made me feel great for a bit, but then I felt horrible later on.'

Fiona

Alcohol affects girls in particularly dangerous ways. Females get drunk quicker, feel the effects faster, get sick more easily and do something stupid more readily.

Binge drinking – where you drink a huge amount in one go – is also dangerous. Thousands of under-sixteens are admitted to hospital every year with alcohol poisoning.

So do yourself a favour: if you're going to try alcohol, do it in moderation, always eat before you drink, be sensible and don't make it a horrible habit.

Quick Fix

If you don't want to be forced by friends to drink, always buy and pour your own drinks wherever you are. Remember, you don't have to tell people what you're drinking or even why you're not drinking.

It's illegal to buy alcoholic drinks if you're under eighteen and illegal to buy cigarettes if you're under sixteen in the UK.

Safe drinking checklist

1. Never drink double measures.
2. Add a soft drink mixer to alcohol to dilute it.
3. Eat while you drink to lessen the effect.
4. Read the alcohol percentage strength on beer bottles – some beers are much stronger than others.
5. Don't be fooled by alcopops – they are stronger than you might think.

HORRIBLE HABIT THREE – JUNK FOOD

You might wonder why junk food is included under horrible habits. Well, eating junk is a habit you need to break if you want to feel good. You may like the taste of high-fat, high-sugar and high-salt food – that's what makes junk so yummy to eat; but all these things are addictive. So the more you eat, the more you'll crave them, and the worse you'll feel. If you're not convinced, try this short quiz.

Do you:

Have less energy then your friends?	Yes/No
Feel tired most of the time?	Yes/No
Find it hard to concentrate?	Yes/No
Feel sleepy and lethargic after lunch?	Yes/No
Need to be woken up in the morning?	Yes/No
Need to lie on the sofa after dinner?	Yes/No
Feel irritable and grumpy for no reason?	Yes/No
Have bad moods?	Yes/No
Feel angry if you can't get your fix of junk snacks?	Yes/No
Always opt for junk over healthier foods?	Yes/No

If you answered yes more than three times, you probably have a junk food horrible habit. Living on chocolate, crisps, burgers, pizza, chips, chicken nuggets, fried chicken, fish and chips, sausage and chips, chips and chips, to give just a few examples, makes you fat and leaves you feeling horrible.

If you love junk food too much to give it up completely, you can still cut down, and make healthier choices like the ones below. That way, you still get a taster of what you like, but without harming your health.

Swap	For
Fizzy colas	Fizzy water
Fruit drinks	Fruit juices (one hundred per cent juice as opposed to a concentrated form of juice)
Ice cream shakes	Fruit smoothies
Pepperoni pizza	Vegetable pizza
Chicken nuggets	Chicken breast
Crisps	Handful of nuts – Brazil nuts and almonds
Milk chocolate	Dark chocolate (eighty per cent cocoa) – less fat and sugar
Chips	Jacket potato (less fat).

HORRIBLE HABIT FOUR – A BAD ATTITUDE

Being healthy is also about your attitude. If you're down on everything and everyone, it's likely you feel depressed and blue most of the time. Hardly surprising when you can't (or won't) see the good in anything. Being negative is a seriously horrible habit!

Your attitude can either be your greatest ally or your worst enemy. You can choose to look on the bright side, be positive and generally focus on good things happening to you, or you can choose to be miserable and wander around feeling gloomy all the time, which will leave you feeling fed up and sad. Of course, none of us are born with a bad mental attitude, so how do we get one? Well, for starters you might get it from:

1. Your parents

This is because how we think is learned from our parents. If they view life negatively, expect the worst to happen and generally teach you to be cautious and wary, that's how you'll think and behave. They are not doing it on purpose – they probably don't even realise they have a horrible habit themselves.

94

2. Your life experience

Disappointments, things going wrong all the time –
if too many bad and upsetting things happen to
you in a row, or your negative experiences out-
weigh your good experiences, it can be easy to
start believing the worst is always going to happen.

3. Your friends

Some people think it's cool to look on the dark
side, or that if you're a downbeat person it
somehow means you're 'deeper' and more
interesting than everyone else. Much of this has
to do with a romantic vision of how we see heroes
and heroines in books and films – but it's not
really true.

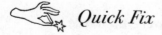 *Quick Fix*

When you're feeling blue, just decide that you're going
to feel good, not bad and make yourself do it. (Yes, you
really can do that.)

A bad mental attitude will leave you feeling drained, lacking energy and unmotivated. This in turn affects your behaviour and the choices you make, which is why your attitude can be bad for your health.

The good news is that to change your attitude, all you need to ask yourself is: what are you getting out of thinking this way?

❀ Does it stop you from feeling disappointed?

❀ Does it make you feel safe?

Then ask yourself which of the following it's stopping you from achieving and doing:

❀ being happy

❀ trying new things

❀ feeling good when you wake up in the morning

❀ feeling hopeful

❀ being motivated

❀ believing in change.

How to get positive

The good thing about any horrible habit is that you can change it by simply deciding to do something about it. Studies show it takes just thirty days to make a new habit, so every day from now on make sure you:

❋ Replace every negative thought with a positive one – even if you don't believe what you're saying (in time you will).

❋ Spend five minutes every day when you wake up thinking positively about the day ahead and imagining good things happening to you.

❋ Think of at least one good thing about a person you don't like.

❋ Challenge yourself to do something anyway, even if you're one hundred per cent sure you can't do it.

❋ Question your behaviour – do you bring your friends down or lift them up?

CHAPTER 5

The A–Z of Body Bliss

A is for Antioxidants

Eating foods rich with antioxidants will help you to look fabulous and feel fabulous for longer. Antioxidants can be found in brightly-coloured vegetables such as tomatoes, peppers and leafy green vegetables, and also in fruits such as oranges, strawberries and kiwi fruit.

B is for Breasts (or boobs)

One of the main signs of puberty is that your breasts start to grow. This can happen at age 11 or younger, or as late as 16 or so – or any time in between! Breasts usually develop slowly over several years, starting with small, hard lumps behind the nipples, and they may feel a bit tender at first. Sometimes one breast grows a bit faster than the other – this is completely normal, and nothing to worry about.

C is for Cellulite

This is squishy skin which looks like orange peel and often appears on the thighs and bottom. Women and celebrity magazines often obsess about it. The beauty industry would have us believe we need all kinds of amazing beauty products to dispel this weird stuff, but really it's just fat collected in a different way under the skin, leading to that dimpled look. Get rid of it with healthy eating and exercise, and get a life!

D is for Dieting

A diet is an eating plan that rules out nearly everything you like to eat! To reach your ideal weight and stay there for ever, you need to zap the diets and eat healthily for life (i.e. a little bit of what you like and a lot of healthy stuff).

E is for Exercise

That's move-your-butt kind of activity! Sixty minutes a day is what you should be doing. Exercise means anything that gets your heart rate up for a sustained period (so running up the stairs once doesn't count, but doing it ten times in a row does).

F is for Fat

Yes, the dreaded 'F' word. The good news is that you need a certain amount of body fat in order to go through puberty. However, as you know already, too much of it is a bad thing, both in terms of self-esteem and health – so see your doctor if you want to know if you need to lose some kilos or not.

G is for Growing

It's something you need to be prepared for, especially between the ages of nine and thirteen. Expect to grow outwards as well as upwards, and remember to give yourself a break while this is happening. It's a bit like blowing up a balloon – the shape you see halfway through isn't necessarily the shape you're going to end up with, so don't panic.

H is for Hormones

Are you suffering from bad moods, spots, irritability and a dip in confidence? If so, blame your hormones. These are the chemicals released from the glands around your body, which activate puberty. Unfortunately they have lots of annoying side effects like the above. But don't despair: they don't last forever and can be combatted with a good diet and plenty of rest. If you really feel bad, see your doctor.

I is for Image

This is how you choose to see yourself. A healthy image means feeling good when you look in the mirror, have your photo taken or bare your body in a communal changing room!

J is for Junk Food

Junk food is fast food or processed food, which tastes yummy because it's packed with fat and sugar and salt. It has little or nothing to offer your body, except making you fat and unhealthy!

L is for Labels

Learn to read labels on food to see what you're really eating. Check out the ingredients – they are listed in order of volume, so if your orange drink says sugar, fructose and then oranges, there is more sugar (fructose is a type of sugar) than anything else in your drink.

M is for Milk

It takes calcium from milk and dairy products to
build strong bones, which means drinking milk is
especially important during the tween and teen
years, when your bones are growing their fastest.
If you're in this age group, you have calcium needs
that you can't make up for later in life.
Unfortunately, fewer than one in ten girls drink
enough milk. To stay healthy for life, you need
three cups of low-fat or fat-free
milk a day plus additional
servings of calcium-rich foods,
such as yogurt, sardines,
broccoli, baked beans and peas.

N is for Nutrition

Your growth at puberty is fuelled by good nutrition,
meaning that if you want to look and feel good,
you have to eat well. On average, a teenage girl
needs two thousand two hundred
calories per day from ages eleven
to eighteen to meet her nutritional
requirements.

O is for Obesity

One in five fifteen-year-olds is now classed as obese – that means seriously overweight. This doesn't have to be you. If you eat healthily and maintain an active life (so you're basically eating less but burning off more energy), you can lose weight and stay fit. If you are overweight or obese, there are things you can do to help yourself, the first being seeking the right help. Visit your doctor, who can refer you to a dietician who will advise you on the best way to lose weight.

P is for Periods

A period is a small amount of bleeding from the vagina which occurs once a month. Most girls will have their first period between the ages of eleven and fourteen, although some will start as early as eight or as late as seventeen.

P is for Puberty

Puberty is the name for the time when your body
begins to develop and change as you move from
being a kid into an adult. It can start any time
between the ages of eight and thirteen.

R is for Relaxing

Everyone needs some down-time to slob, hang out
and generally just rest up – and, surprisingly,
being lazy now and again is
good for your mental health.
So make sure you take time out
from your life and try not to
obsess about problems at
school or at home.

S is for Stress

Stress manifests itself
in many ways – as
low feelings or the
blues, crying, anger
or even illness. Stress
is the direct result of
pressures in a particular area of life – for example,
at school, in a relationship, or at home. The way
to solve it is to tackle the causes by being honest
about how you feel, instead of bottling it all up
inside – write it all down in a diary, and try to find
someone you trust to talk to. If you still feel bad,
see a doctor.

T is for Tiredness

Tiredness is common during puberty simply
because the body is growing and so you get
exhausted faster. Think how much new babies
sleep when they're growing! The key is to make
sure you get eight to ten hours of sleep a night,
and eat a healthy diet (sugar and fat make you feel
even more tired).

U is for UVA/UVB Rays

Ultraviolet rays are broken down into two types – UVB are the rays that burn your skin, and UVA rays are the ones that attack the skin on a deeper level. Both can cause skin cancer. In order to protect yourself you need a sunscreen that offers protection from both – read the back of the bottle!

W is for Wrinkles

Think you won't get them for decades? Well, think again! Sun damage begins in your childhood and teenage years, so look after your skin and protect it from the sun NOW.

Y is for Yo-Yo Dieting

Yo-Yo dieting refers to the process of losing and gaining weight in repeated cycles – and is bad news. It's bad for your health and skin, makes you obsessed with food, and generally is about as far away from healthy eating as you can get.

Zzzz . . . Sleep

Do you have trouble waking in the mornings and feel like a zombie by mid-afternoon? If so, the chances are you're sleep deprived. For optimum health, you need at least eight to ten hours every night, with no really late nights, and no big sleep-ins at weekends.

Bye-bye
body blips!

Now you know that looking and feeling gorgeous is within your power. Whether it's getting fit or eating well, changing your attitude or ditching those horrible habits, it's up to you to make it happen.

You can do it!

Finding out more

Here are some recommended books, helplines and websites which can give you more information and advice.

Everything You Ever Wanted to Ask About . . . Periods

Tricia Kreitman, Dr Fiona Finlay and
Dr Rosemary Jones
Piccadilly Press
A reassuring and informative book all about periods.

ChildLine

Tel: 0800 1111
www.childline.org.uk
You can call the free helpline at any time of day or night and the number won't show up on the bill.

BULLYING

www.bullying.co.uk

Tel: 020 7378 1446
Includes a 24-hour online bullying helpline:
help@bullying.co.uk

SMOKING

NHS Helpline: 0800 169 0 169
www.givingupsmoking.co.uk

SPORTS

Sports organisations

England: www.sportengland.org
Scotland: www.sportscoltand.org.uk
Wales: sports-council-wales.co.uk
Northern Ireland: www.sportni.org
Loads of ideas on how and where to get active in your area.

SPOTS

Acne Support Group

www.stopspots.org
Expert advice on skin problems.

Index

Also from Piccadilly Press

Everything You Ever Wanted to Ask About... Periods

*Tricia Kreitman, Dr Fiona Finlay
and Dr Rosemary Jones*

Do you have a million questions about periods? Or can't you even bear to think about them? Talking about this subject can be difficult, but this book comes to the rescue with answers to real questions that thousands of real girls have already asked.

- How do you know when your periods are about to start?
- What will it really be like?
- Who do you tell?
- What do you use?
- Will you be different?

A highly readable and reassuring guide, approved by the Family Planning Association.

ISBN 978 1 85340 672 0

Also from Piccadilly Press

Is Anyone's Family as Mad as Mine?

A SURVIVAL GUIDE FOR TEENAGERS

Kathryn Lamb

**Families. At best, they cramp your style.
At worst, they drive you completely mad!**

But there is hope! All you need is the right
approach and a little inside knowledge and you
can stay sane. This book provides all the tactics
you'll ever need to deal with the most frustrating
of families. No matter what the occasion or what
the issue, you'll be able to silence your siblings
and placate your parents while keeping your
social life intact.

ISBN 978 1 85340 883 0

Also from Piccadilly Press

Do the Right Thing
A teenager's guide to surviving any social situation

Jane Goldman

Ever wanted the floor to swallow you up?

Revised and updated, this hugely popular and
helpful book is back in print, packed with even
more advice on how to cope with every kind of
embarrassing situation. Whether you're eating
out, giving presents, telling your friend some
home truths or failing to flush the loo at a party,
Jane Goldman offers sensible and funny
strategies to get you through.

Now includes web and email etiquette.

ISBN 978 1 85340 894 6